Contents

What to Do

Choose a face

Remember the colour you have chosen.

When you see your face on the page, you are the LEADER.

The LEADER reads the text in the speech bubbles.

There are extra words and questions to help you on the teacher's whiteboard. The LEADER reads these aloud.

When you see this stop sign, the LEADER reads it aloud.

STOP
My predictions were right/wrong because . . .

You might need:

- to look at the WORD HELP on pages 20–22;
- to look at the LOCATION HELP on page 23;
- an atlas.

If you are the LEADER, follow these steps:

1 PREDICT

Think about what is on the page.

- Say to your group:

"I am looking at this page and I think it is going to be about…"

- Tell your group:

"Read the page to yourselves."

2 CLARIFY

Talk about words and their meaning.

- Say to your group:

"Are there any words you don't know?"

"Is there anything else on the page you didn't understand?"

- Talk about the words and their meanings with your group.

- Read the whiteboard.

Let's check:

- Ask your group to find the LET'S CHECK word in the WORD HELP on pages 20–22. Ask them to read the meaning of the word aloud.

3 ASK QUESTIONS

Talk about how to find out more.

- Say to your group:

"Who has a question about what we have read?"

- Question starters are: how…, why…, when…, where…, what…, who…

- Read the question on the whiteboard and talk about it with your group.

4 SUMMARISE

Think about who and what the story was mainly about.

This page was mainly about fact fact

When you get to pages 16–17, you can talk to a partner or write and draw on your own.

  or

Volcano Detectives

I am looking at this page and I think it is going to be about... because...

Some volcanoes are **extinct**. Others are sleeping or **dormant** and could have been for hundreds of years. These dormant volcanoes could wake up. When they do, they are active. They could **erupt** at anytime.

Some scientists have the job of learning all about volcanoes. They are like **detectives** who look for clues. Their clues, however, are near the volcanoes.

Are there any words you don't know?

Let's check: erupt

Who has a question about what we have read?

What type of clues do you think that scientists might find in the rocks?

Stanley Williams is a 'volcano detective'. He looks for clues in the rocks.

This page was mainly about fact fact

STOP
My predictions were right/wrong because . . .

How? Why? When?

Scientists need to find out how and why volcanoes erupt. They also have to try to find out when one might erupt again. This is a very important part of the scientist's job.

There are hundreds of volcanoes around the world. If the scientists say a volcano won't erupt and it does, then many people could die.

I am looking at this page and I think it is going to be about... because...

Are there any words you don't know?

Let's check: spewed

Who has a question about what we have read?

How do you think scientists might know when a volcano is going to erupt?

This volcano is in Chile. After thousands of years it started erupting for the first time. It **spewed ash**, **gas** and hot rock into the air.

If a Volcano Wakes Up

I am looking at this page and I think it is going to be about… because…

Sometimes, scientists have to go very close to, or even into, a volcano. This is a very dangerous job.

Like a sleeping bear, a dormant volcano might just 'wake up' at any moment. The ground might shake. It could be very, very hot. Rocks could fly like bombs. There could be **poisonous** gas in the air. This gas could **choke** anyone who breathed it in.

Are there any words you don't know?

Let's check: poisonous

Who has a question about what we have read?

Why do you think a volcano could be described as a sleeping bear?

These scientists are carrying out tests on the edge of a volcano.

STOP

My predictions were right/wrong because . . .

This page was mainly about

fact

fact

A Volcano Wakes Up

I am looking at this page and I think it is going to be about… because…

Stanley Williams is a scientist. He works with people from around the world. They study dormant volcanoes to find out when they might erupt.

One day, Stanley and his team were on the edge of a volcano. Suddenly, the ground began to shake. There was a huge **explosion**. Hot rocks went flying through the air.

Are there any words you don't know?

Let's check: explosion

Who has a question about what we have read?

What do you think might happen to Stanley and his team?

A Terrible Day

I am looking at this page and I think it is going to be about… because…

The rocks were flying around Stanley. One rock hit him on the head and **crushed** some of his bones. His clothes caught fire. He was hit by rocks again and again.

When rescuers found Stanley he was covered in ash and blood. He was burned badly. He had broken legs and a broken nose. Stanley, however, was lucky. Many of his team did not **survive**.

Are there any words you don't know?

Let's check:
survive

Who has a question about what we have read?

How do you think Stanley's clothes caught fire?

Fire breaks out on Galeras Volcano. It is caused by the hot rocks that the volcano spews out.

People are trying to escape from the erupting volcano.

This page was mainly about fact fact

STOP
My predictions were right/wrong because . . .

Watching Volcanoes

Millions of people live near dormant volcanoes. Sometimes there is no **warning**. These volcanoes can erupt at any time.

Scientists like Stanley have a very important but dangerous job. They are trying to find out if these **rumbling** giants will become active or not.

Scientists climb into a mountain's **crater**.

Another volcano rumbles over a large city and **threatens** to explode.

This page was mainly about

fact

fact

STOP
My predictions were right/wrong because . . .

Something to Think About

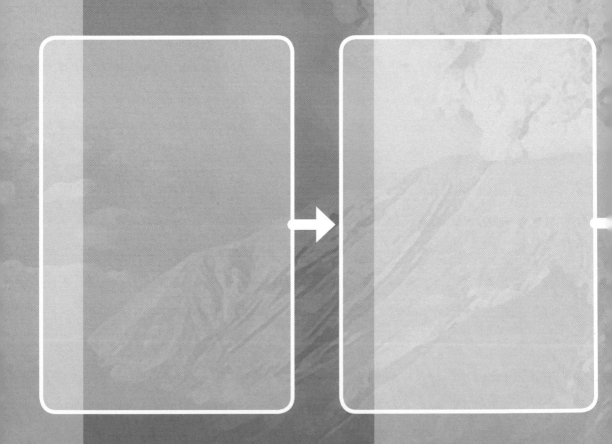

Think about what happens when a dormant volcano wakes up. Talk about your ideas with a partner, write them down or draw them.

Do You Need to Find an Answer?

You could go to . . .

Library >

Expert >

Internet >

Do You Want to Find Out More?

You could look in books or on the internet. These key words could help you:

active volcanoes

dormant volcanoes

extinct volcanoes

Stanley Williams, volcanologist

volcanologists

Word Help

Dictionary

active	an active volcano may erupt soon or is already erupting
ash	powdered rock and glass that erupts from a volcano
choke	to stop someone from breathing
crater	a round hole in the shape of a V caused by a volcanic eruption
crushed	damaged something by pressing it hard
detectives	people who look for clues and gather information
dormant	a dormant volcano is not erupting, but is not extinct
erupt	to shoot out lava or gas

explosion	a loud bang made by something bursting or blowing up
extinct	an extinct volcano will never erupt again
gas	something that has no shape and can spread out in the air
poisonous	something that can cause harm because it contains poison
rumbling	making a deep, heavy sound
spewed	forced out liquid
survive	to manage to stay alive
threatens	shows that something bad might happen
warning	a sign that something bad might happen

Word Help

Thesaurus

badly	severely, seriously
broken	shattered, injured
clues	signs, evidence, hints
dangerous	unsafe, risky
huge	vast, colossal, gigantic, great
important	valuable
shake	tremble, quiver, quake
team	squad, group

Location Help

Where the Volcanoes Are

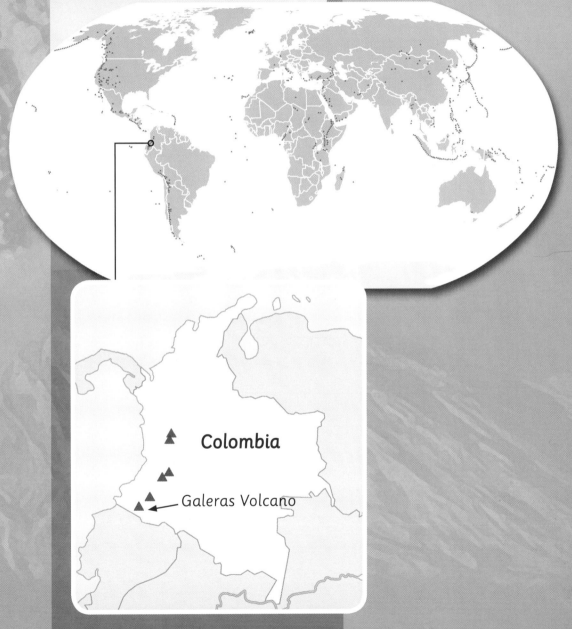

Colombia

Galeras Volcano

Index